THE
Date Night
Questions
EXPERIENCE
Marriage and Martinis

Danielle and Adam Silverstein

ISBN 979-8-9871479-1-7

Contents

Introduction

In our twenty-plus years together, Adam and I have always made date night a priority. Once we had kids, this time together became even more important, and the regularity of being together and reconnecting on the weekend may have even saved our marriage a few times. While making the time to be alone together is good and an important first step, I've realized that these date nights could have been taken to the next level as a time for us to really bond and communicate. I wish that we'd used that alone time in a deeper and more meaningful way. How is it that we went out almost every single weekend for three or four hours and yet, I still never realized how incredibly stressed Adam was about our financial situation? How did he not know how self-conscious I was when we would go home to have sex and I would have to take my clothes off? The whole time, we could have been focusing more intently on one another's needs and desires and nurturing our relationship. There could have been this amazing balance between light-hearted fun and more in-depth consideration and understanding. Instead, we kept our interactions and conversations superficial and predictable, as a means to remain complacent and comfortable. Honestly, I think we were scared. We didn't want to ruin the fun of our Saturday night by possibly bringing up a discussion that would cause a disagreement. When an argument did occur on a date night, it became an explosion.

The truth was that we didn't know how to communicate without there being a winner and a loser. We didn't know how to talk about the important, more serious details of our life together without placing blame. It never occurred to us that it is possible to discuss vital issues and decisions in a way that was productive while also deepening intimacy and connection. That was, until we started planning and recording a podcast. If we were going to be successful and produce content that related to and effectively helped other couples, we were going to have no choice but to learn how to speak to one another without constant fighting and disappointment. Over the past two-and-a- half years, this is what we've worked so hard to improve. With practice and the help of incredible therapists and experts, we've learned to structure the questions we ask one another in each episode in a manner that generates laughter, debate, sharing, and growth. Does every recording end without animosity and resentment? Of course not. But I never thought we would come as far as we have. I am so proud of the work we've done and the new strategies and practices we've embraced.

Now, we're sharing many of the best and most effective topics and questions with you. You have already taken the first step by purchasing this ebook. Our hope for the date night questions is for you to use these questions as a catalyst for your own personal growth as a couple. You don't need a podcast to break down life together and explore all facets of the universe, love, parenting, work, sex, and everything in between. We've spent hundreds of hours experimenting with different ingredients to produce a more productive formula for healthier communication, and we finally feel confident and so excited to share the recipe. Now, you can start adding your own personal spices and flavors to work on your own relationship.

Sit down, relax, and have some appetizers, wine, or coffee. Keep an open mind and heart while getting into the flow of embracing one another's ideas, opinions, dreams and goals. Complete the topics in order, out of order, backwards....however you prefer! Most importantly, get ready to laugh, maybe cry a little, experience deeper emotional and physical intimacy, and understand one another in a way that you haven't before.

Welcome to Volume One of the Marriage and Martinis' Date Night Question Experience.

Before you begin....

Communication is an ever-evolving, complicated process. When composing these questions, our intentions were to make them as generous and gentle in tone as possible. However, every couple has its trigger spots, and what might be a benign topic for one set of partners might provoke an argument or pick at festering wounds for another. When looking through the topics and deciding upon the one that best matches your mood for a certain date night or occasion, think about a few key points:

1. Is this a sensitive topic for our relationship? If so, is the setting of our date night appropriate for a more intense discussion? Is this something we should be discussing in a public setting, or should we be in the privacy of our own living room? What can we do to prepare for what possibly might become a more heated conversation (albeit an important and hopefully constructive one) in advance?

2. Decide that you're both willing to get a little silly and be open-minded when it comes to the small bonding challenges (as well as the questions). Channel your inner-child who loved projects and crafts; your middle school self whose outlets of expressions included things like mix-tapes and magazine collages. Check your "cool" at the door and go for "vulnerable." Also, help to create a safe and accepting space for your partner to do the same.

3. Remember that you are a team! At the heart of all of this, you are both here for the same reason: to make life as wonderful, successful, and joyous together, individually, and for each other as possible. It might be worth it to come up with a gentle

keyword or phrase, a designated special touch, or some strategy to diffuse, re-center and reconnect if the dialogue starts to diverge in a direction that's hurtful or unproductive. This is a whole conversation in itself that's worth having. "What can we both do to make these conversations as impactful and loving as possible?"

4. The questions are meant to be asked by one partner and answered by the other and then you switch roles, so each partner gets to ask and answer the questions. Remember to be patient, kind, courteous, and generous when your partner is answering. Being the receiver of these answers and anecdotes is just as important (if not more) than being the one answering. You have the opportunity to create a space of safety, openness, respect, and love. Take that role and make the most of it.

Remember This Acronym:

D are to be vulnerable

A ttentive listening

T ake turns talking

E mpathic response

The Story of Us

We all have a love story. Sometimes we need to go back to that story to spark some of those emotions that have been buried beneath the baggage of everyday life: work, finances, parenting, health issues, family drama, and everything else that gets thrown our way. Stripping it all away to get back to the purity, magic, and bliss of falling in love helps us revisit the reasons we chose one another in the first place. We've told the story of how we met so many times, that I'm not even sure what's real and what's altered at this point. Malcolm Gladwell says that every time we take a story off the shelf, we corrupt it a little bit. However, if we don't take it down from the shelf, it might be forgotten. We each have our own version of each and every story, and that's how it becomes ours.

I love to tell people about the details of when we were introduced by our mutual friend, Rebecca, who has always been this bright ray of sunshine in our lives. Adam was the quintessential "bad boy," always with a cigarette hanging out of his mouth, and girls from miles around would warn their friends about him. He also had eyes that seemed to pierce straight into your soul. That was the first thing that most people noticed about him. Our first date in high school together resulted in us going back to his dorm room (he was at boarding school), and hiding me in his closet from the RA. Later that evening, he covered my neck in hickies, resulting in my expulsion from a very important field hockey game the next day. These were probably all signals that Adam was trouble. But I was highly attracted to, and am still excited by the bad boy in him that keeps life adventurous. It's simultaneously been the most problematic aspect of our relationship; the fact that we both have some of that "rebellious kid" in us that never dissipated.

There are so many layers to our story. It's multi-faceted and fun. The best part? It's all ours. No matter what transpires in our relationship, that unique story will always be there as a reminder that the foundation of our life together is rooted in love, appreciation, physical and emotional attraction. Channeling those giddy, intoxicating emotions by revisiting the beginning stages of falling in love is important. Underneath all the layers of stress, expectation and responsibility are still those two young kids who want to be fun, carefree, and a little....bad. The heaviness of the years between us and that fresh, excited couple is real. But with a little push and some deep nostalgia, we can still unlock those same thrilling feelings of infatuation and passion.

Date Night Questions

The Story of Us

1. What is the most unique aspect about our "meeting" story? Which aspect of it do you love most?

_____

_____

_____

_____

_____

2. Three words that best describe that first interaction:

_____

_____

_____

3. Were there unexpected circumstances involved in our meeting; circumstances which, had they gone differently, may have resulted in us never having met, or at least not in the same time and place? Explain.

_____

_____

_____

_____

_____

_____

4. Is there a specific quote or statement that I said that sticks out in your mind? What about it is so memorable as it applies to us as a couple?

_____

_____

_____

_____

_____

5. What qualities/characteristics do you still see in me that have not changed much since our first meeting? In what ways do I still manifest these traits?

_____

_____

_____

_____

_____

_____

6. Is there an aspect of each of us, our personalities and/or be-
   haviors that you would love to reignite, that has faded or gotten lost in the chaos and burdens of life?

_____

_____

_____

_____

_____

7. If you could go back and tell that couple one thing that night
   so they could better prepare for their future, what would it be?
   What advice or insight did we both lack but from which we
   could have greatly benefitted?

_____

_____

_____

8. A movie is being written about our love story. What is the title? Who plays you? Who plays me? What's it rated?

The Story Of Us Challenge

Set the timer for five minutes (minimum) and separately write every single detail about the two of you meeting that you can remember. Be as detailed as possible about the time of day, place, what you were wearing, who was there, if there was music playing. After five minutes, read your accounts back to one another and then compare/contrast.

Life Is An Obstacle Course

One of the first posts I ever wrote on instagram was titled, "I wish someone had told me...." I wish someone had told me that marriage isn't actually 50/50. I wish someone had told me that "hard" doesn't necessarily mean "bad." In actuality, I'm sure along the way people did hint much of this to me, but I didn't truly understand how many roadblocks and obstacles emerge simply due to being an adult (a term I still think should not apply to me). Adam and I have been blessed in so many ways, and I don't want to appear ungrateful. I have tremendous gratitude. But I also have felt so blindsided many times: professionally, as a parent, personally, and in my marriage.

Whether it was discovering the shocking truth about our finances, moving six times within the same town, a debilitating bout with OCD that forced me to move out with Adam and in with my parents for months, my son unexpectedly spending a week in the nicu after birth, a miscarriage, postpartum depression, etc., we've dealt with our share of adversity. Hardships are all relative. But, they are all real and deserve to be treated as such no matter the severity. We don't need comparison, we just need support.

Life truly is an obstacle course. I think that with each hurdle we developed thicker skin and a greater appreciation for life and the skills and capacity to heal. I have filled my "emotional toolbelt" with so many helpful coping mechanisms and self-care essentials. However, it has not been easy and I cannot pretend to have survived each with the utmost grace and courage. There were certainly struggles I have gone through kicking, screaming, and complaining. However, I am proud of Adam and me for getting through it all and continuing to grow and thrive.

I've equated Adam's and my life together to a game of Chutes and Ladders. There are times when the ladder of success seemed so easy that we jumped to the next rung with little effort or burden. But man, those slides back down to rock bottom sure feel like they're 1980's playground style; made of metal and scalding on a blazing hot day. Looking back, I wouldn't change those obstacles for anything. They truly have made us the grateful, accepting, empathetic, hard-working, people we are today. I do hope that the struggles that lay ahead are of less consequence than those behind us. However, I do know that whatever comes our way, we'll be better equipped to deal with it than we ever have been before.

Date Night Questions

Life Is An Obstacle Course

1. What are three obstacles in your own life you would never have anticipated or by which you felt completely blindsided? What did you learn from them?

   _____

   _____

   _____

   _____

   _____

2. Is there something, a resource or practice in your life, that has consistently helped you to cope with those hard times? Is there a form of self-care that you turn to for healing, realignment and support?

   _____

   _____

   _____

_____

_____

_____

3. What is a lesson, strategy, skill or practice you wish you had been taught or told growing up, either by your parents, teachers, mentors, etc. that could have really helped get you through these times and relieved some of the burden?

_____

_____

_____

_____

_____

4. How has being a team and having one another helped you through one of these times? Is there a specific incident you can remember when I really helped you to get through?

_____

_____

_____

_____

5. How can we work even better moving forward to tackle these issues? What do you need more of from me? What do you think I need more of from you?

_____

_____

_____

_____

_____

6. If you could snap your fingers and take away one challenge you know I deal with and causes me stress, what would it be?

_____

_____

_____

_____

_____

The Obstacle Course Challenge:

Fill out the following Yes/No/Maybe checklist of resources and activities (yes if it's something you would be willing to try, maybe for something you would consider and about which you would like to learn more, and no for something that does not interest you.) Once each of you has filled out your own checklist, go over the options to see which methods are the most plausible for you. If there's a method that interests you that we've missed, feel free to add it in the blank spaces.

Bonus: Choose one method on which you both agree and take the next step in your research. Book a session, download an app, google more information....just something to get the ball rolling.

Yes, No, Maybe Challenge

LIFE IS AN OBSTACLE COURSE

	YES	NO	MAYBE
Download a meditation app such as Headspace or Calm	☐	☐	☐
Counseling app such as Better Help or Lasting	☐	☐	☐
Yoga	☐	☐	☐
Journaling	☐	☐	☐
Go on a retreat such as a place like Kripalu	☐	☐	☐
Starting a daily gratitude text back and forth listing 3 things for which we're each grateful	☐	☐	☐
Read (or listen to) a book such as *Unf*ck Yourself*, *Atomic Habits*, or the *Year Of Yes*, and discuss	☐	☐	☐
Acupuncture	☐	☐	☐
Find a Ted Talk about overcoming adversity (there are dozens). Watch it together and then discuss.	☐	☐	☐

Yes, No, Maybe Challenge

LIFE IS AN OBSTACLE COURSE

	YES	NO	MAYBE
Download a meditation app such as Headspace or Calm	☐	☐	☐
Counseling app such as Better Help or Lasting	☐	☐	☐
Yoga	☐	☐	☐
Journaling	☐	☐	☐
Go on a retreat such as a place like Kripalu	☐	☐	☐
Starting a daily gratitude text back and forth listing 3 things for which we're each grateful	☐	☐	☐
Read (or listen to) a book such as *Unf*ck Yourself*, *Atomic Habits*, or the *Year Of Yes*, and discuss	☐	☐	☐
Acupuncture	☐	☐	☐
Find a Ted Talk about overcoming adversity (there are dozens). Watch it together and then discuss.	☐	☐	☐

Let's Talk About Libido

I started having sex late in life in comparison to my friends. I was twenty-years-old. I would equate my first few times to "sugar-free chocolate cake." Yes, it was chocolate (yum) but, it was also "sugar-free" (eh). Adam, on the other hand, had several partners before he met (and re-met) me. I don't know the exact number, but it was a lot. When we got together at 22-years-old, he was my second partner and I was ready to have sex in the mad, passionate way I had always seen in the movies and on TV. And I was ready to have it ALL THE TIME. Adam still lived with his parents (and somehow despite this fact, I still wanted to have sex with him), but I didn't care who was home, how thin the walls were, what time of day it was....I. Just. Wanted. It.

Skip ahead a couple of decades to a full-time job, marriage, three kids, financial stress, mental illness and SSRI's, self-esteem issues, a pandemic, (should I keep going?). Let's just say the tables have turned 180 degrees, and Adam is currently the one who initiates sex more often. There have also been periods of such extreme sexual drought, that I wasn't sure my garden would ever get watered and cared for again. My lady parts have wilted from lack of sunlight and attention more than once. Honestly, I've been ok with those breaks.

I truly believe in ebbs and flows; During all three of my full-term pregnancies, I could count on one hand the number the times we had sex or were even intimate in any capacity. We have accepted that there will be times when life doesn't allow for the intimacy we wish was possible. Maybe not all couples go through this, but for us, it's a reality. On the other hand, we have paid attention to the details of our schedule and connection that result in the best, most passionate sex and intimacy between us. A few factors we've learned to be attuned to and pay attention to:

Danielle's List:

A. I know my body and cycle. When I'm ovulating, I tend to feel sexier and want sex more. For us, those are good nights to plan date nights.

B. I feel much more turned on when I feel like Adam wants me and has been giving me signals that I turn him on.

C. I'm turned off when Adam stays up later than me to watch a movie and then wakes me to have sex, because I feel like he isn't being sensitive to my needs for a full night's sleep.

D. Sex when the kids are still awake is too stressful. Either late night (before I fall asleep), when the kids are sleeping out, or at a hotel works best and keeps me the most relaxed.

E. The more overwhelmed I'm feeling in life, the more my libido decreases. If I feel seen, understood and helped by Adam, I am much more likely to want to be intimate.

Adam's List:

A. A date night is foreplay. Getting "dressed up" and getting out of the house for a night enhances the anticipation of amazing sex.

B. If there's any feeling of disconnect between us, and our relationship has become like "ships passing in the night," I have no real interest in sex.

C. Sex at home is stressful. Between the kids and the dogs, there's no real moment that's just ours to enjoy. A weekend at a hotel is worth whatever it costs for us. We need that to realign and jumpstart the excitement.

D. I'm much more turned on when Danielle is having a "nice" day, and hasn't been stressed and yelling at everyone in our family all day.

E. Trying new things in bed is a huge turn on. This is fairly new to us and it's been fun changing things up. Forever is a long time, so keeping it interesting has been key for me.

Date Night Questions

Let's Talk About Libido

1. We're planning a weekend together just the two of us, to re-connect and spark more intimacy. What does a weekend like that look like to you? (be as detailed as possible)

_____

_____

_____

_____

_____

_____

2. Answer each of the following:

   a. Favorite body part of mine:

   _____

   b. Favorite body part you like to be touched by me:

   _____

   c. Sexiest movie:

   _____

d. Sexiest song or soundtrack:

_____

e. Sexiest or most romantic memory of the two of us:

_____

f. Location/setting that would definitely help put you in the mood:

_____

g. Smell that you associate with sex:

_____

3. How would you say both of our libidos have affected our sex life over the years? How might we work on "revving up" our sex life some?

_____

_____

_____

_____

_____

_____

4. Something specific that I could do more of to help make you feel wanted or desired?

_____

_____

5. What is something that turns you on when you think about it?

6. What is something that turns you off when you think about it?

7. Time of day that's most enjoyable for you to have sex.

_____

_____

_____

_____

_____

8. Three factors which, when aligned, make you feel the most comfortable and relaxed for intimacy (see mine and Adam's list above as a guide if needed).

_____

_____

_____

_____

_____

The Libido Challenge:
Seven minutes in heaven

Head to a closet, the back seat of your car, the bathroom, pantry, or outside the house behind the bushes. Set a timer for seven minutes and just make out with no expectations of what happens next.

Bonus: While you're making out, ask your partner to do one thing specifically that will make you feel good. *Note: If you are too uncomfortable to ask one another verbally while making out, take a moment beforehand to write your requests on pieces of paper or post-it notes and exchange them. Don't knock it. It works.

The Mental Load

Here we are at the topic that has probably caused the most contention in Adam and my marriage. For us, this struggle dates all the back to the year 2001, when we were living in our first condo. Adam was working and I was studying for exams. There was a pot in the sink that we both thought the other person should wash. That's it. That's the fight. A pot in the sink that both of us thought we were far too busy and overwhelmed to clean, and therefore, the other person should do it because their life was easier and less overwhelming. I wish I could tell you that was a fight of sheer immaturity and we've grown greatly since then. While these disputes have morphed into who should have to drive to basketball practice or whose turn it is to discipline our son for staying up too late playing video games, at its core, the struggle is the same. Each of us thinks we bear a larger brunt of the responsibilities. This tug-of-war style conflict never ends well. Inevitably, both of us wind up in the mud.

As my therapist recently pointed out, it doesn't really matter who believes they carry the heavier burden of family life and work. If one or both partner(s) feels like they're drowning and can't manage it all, it's time to re-evaluate roles and figure out how to make things more feasible. Life Coach Amy Alpert has a brilliant analogy: just like kids empty their candy bags at Halloween to swap and trade, the same can be done with chores and responsibilities between couples (and delegating to kids, family members, paid services, etc). Put it "all out on the table," and see if there's anything you could trade, even temporarily, to break the monotony, and support one another in a new way.

There isn't anything sexy about this conversation. However, having a partner who demonstrates they are willing to discuss hard topics as a means to make life better for the other person is actually an incredibly attractive gesture. As I once so profoundly stated, "acts of service in the domestic realm often lead to, well, more frequent acts of service in the sexual realm." It turned out to be a controversial statement, but I stand by it. The good news is that research about this topic is finally becoming a priority, and strategies to improve this strain on relationships are being shared in books such as Fair Play by Eve Rodsky, Drop The Ball by Tiffany Dufu, and All The Rage by Darcy Lockman. For the moment, it's extremely important during this discussion to remember that ultimately, you're actually both on the same team with shared goals for a happier, safer, more prosperous life.

Date Night Questions

The Mental Load

1. What are three "small-ish" tasks I do around the house or with family life that you appreciate but maybe don't say it enough?

_____

_____

_____

_____

_____

2. What are three "small-ish" tasks you do around the house or with family life that you think go unnoticed and for which you would like a bit more appreciation?

_____

_____

_____

_____

3. Do you believe in "Choreplay?" (Are you turned on/think it's sexy seeing me taking care of us and our family? Anything specifically?)

_____

_____

_____

_____

_____

4. If you could (realistically) get rid of one task in which you're in charge, what would it be and why? Is there a way I could help take that burden off of you?

_____

_____

_____

_____

_____

5. How does thinking about everything you need to get done make you feel? What task/responsibility are you the most anxious about? How does it affect you on a daily basis? What do you think would make it better?

_____

_____

_____

_____

_____

6. What form of communication do you think would be best when we need to discuss things that need to get done/upcoming events/responsibilities?

a. A weekly "meeting" once a week either with coffee or wine/cocktails? If so, when and where should it be?

b. A Google Doc or some document that we both check throughout the week and can assign/choose tasks that need to be done.

c. A blackboard or white board in the kitchen or office where we write out the week and decide who is going to do what.

d. The Fair Play Card Deck

e. Some other form of communication? If so, what?

The Mental Load Small challenge:

Get a package of index cards or cut up sheets of paper into card-sized pieces. Each of you take ten of them. Privately, write a (reasonable) task concerning domestic/family labor and responsibility about which you feel stress. Afterwards, lay them all out and see if there is anything you're willing to swap for the week. Is there something your partner laid out that makes more sense for you to be doing or vice versa? Is there a task that you can delegate to someone else? Use these cards as a roadmap to making life a bit less stressful. Make as many swaps/delegate as many tasks for the week as you would like. *For a more detailed version of this challenge, purchase the amazing Fair Play Card Deck, created by Eve Rodsky.

Bonus: Set a meeting time in one week to discuss how it went and re-evaluate.

Gratitude and Appreciation

I'll never forget for Adam's 30th birthday, I was planning a surprise party for him. Mia, our oldest child, was two-and-a-half, and I was newly pregnant with our second child, dealing with first-trimester morning sickness while also chasing around a toddler. I was tired. I worked for weeks (maybe months) planning a celebratory casino night in our backyard. I reached out to old friends Adam hadn't seen in years, and planned a catered BBQ with tastings of Adam's favorite wines. It really was an awesome night.

The next morning, Adam came downstairs after sleeping late, hugged me, and handed me a gift. "I know how hard you've been working planning this party. I just want you to know that I've seen everything you've been doing and I appreciate it so much." Those words alone were more than enough. The fact that he got me a beautiful present, a gorgeous clutch that I still use to this day, was an added bonus. I realize that gratitude runs so much deeper than casino parties and designer handbags. But in that moment, there was this powerful feeling of being seen: the details, the multi-tasking, the exhaustion and nausea - it had not gone unnoticed.

I wish I could say that moments of sheer appreciation have been consistent in our relationship. We have sporadically given or planned surprise gifts of grandiosity for one another. However, when daily life is in a whirlwind of chaos, rarely do we stop to remind one another how grateful we are for the everyday actions: the ones that feel mundane and expected, but are crucial to the functioning and success of our lives together. On the contrary, it's usually more of an argument about who does more and is more exhausted.

There are certain acts that I do keep in the back of my mind for when Adam and I are fighting, or it seems like intentions are more selfish than generous; the tug-of-war of things like time, sleep, and even money. A few of the moments I keep in my "memory box of gratitude," when I need to remember that Adam and I are truly on the same team, and I need to stop and just be grateful:

- The moment I asked him to start a podcast together. His response is one I will never forget. I was sure he would say no. I was convinced he would not take me seriously. And yet, here we are, two and a half years later, all because he believed in my idea and said yes.

- How supportive Adam always was whenever I made a decision that went "against the grain," concerning pregnancy and new motherhood. Needing to be on SSRI's and deciding not to even try breastfeeding were two decisions (while not the right ones for everyone) that I felt I needed to make in my gut. The support and understanding I received from Adam on issues pertaining to my mental health have been incredible. I know there could have been added stress from contrasting opinions. I have been so blessed to have a partner who is non-judgmental about issues that are crucial to my well-being.

Date Night Questions

Gratitude and Appreciation

1. What three moments or reasons come to mind to keep in your "memory box of gratitude" when you think about our time together? What are some moments when you have been especially grateful for having me by your side? (Double points if it's something you've never told me before.)

_____

_____

_____

_____

_____

_____

2. Gretchen Rubin says that from the moment we open our eyes in the morning and our feet hit the floor, we already have a reason to be grateful. We are alive. For which small instances throughout your day that often go unrecognized are you most grateful?

_____

_____

_____

_____

_____

_____

3. Something for which you're grateful for from each category (be as specific as possible):

   a. Sound:

   _____

   b. Smell:

   _____

   c. Sight:

   _____

   d. Touch:

   _____

   e. Taste:

   _____

   f. Something about how your body works:

   _____

   g. Something about how your mind works:

   _____

h. Person you wish you saw more:

_____

i. Something in nature:

_____

j. Place:

_____

k. Something you own:

_____

l. Taste:

_____

m. Invention:

_____

n. Luxury you take for granted:

_____

o. Something/someone that inspires you:

_____

p. Regarding what you're most grateful for concerning me:

_____

q. Daily task I do that goes unnoticed:

_____

r. Aspect of my personality:

_____

s. Something about my physical presence:

_____

t. Something that makes me a great partner:

_____

u. One way you can show me more appreciation moving
forward:

_____

Day Gratitude challenge:

Starting right now, decide on a method and time of day you both prefer for expressing gratitude (you can each pick what's more comfortable for you). Then for the next seven days, choose one thing each day about which you're grateful concerning your partner and/or your life together, and let them know (try not to repeat what you have discussed here).

Bonus: Keep the daily expression of gratitude going longer than seven days, and let it transform into a life practice. Some recommended methods for expressing your daily appreciation:

1. Text chain
2. Post-it notes left somewhere visible for the other person
3. A shared journal
4. Face to face
5. Something else?

Nostalgia and Upbringing

From the outside, it seems like Adam's and my upbringing would have been very similar. We're the same religion, grew up in nearby suburbs in the same state, our parents both had strong marriages, we are both youngest children, and he and I attended rival private schools. However, I think the details and intricacies of how each of us was raised, as well as our personal expectations for what the roles of a husband and wife are supposed to be based on those of our parents, have weighed heavily on our relationship. Assumptions about issues like traditional gender roles in marriage, how money and possessions will influence our life, and what "makes a house a home," are just a few of the standards from our own upbringing that we held on to causing much contention in our own relationship. I wish that from the beginning we had formulated our own ideas and practices rather than just recreating those of our parents. However, it wasn't even something that we were doing consciously. It took years to figure out that so many of our fights weren't even about our discrepancies and differing opinions, it was about those of our parents and the way they raised us. Just because those were the homes in which we grew up, didn't mean we had to replicate every facet of their beliefs and choices.

We have since worked so hard to create a balance between the older traditions, values, and routines of our parents and grandparents that work for our lifestyle, while letting go of the ones that don't. This process is as tricky as it sounds. It takes a lot of communicating, patience, sacrifice and acceptance. Mostly though, it takes a strong understanding that it's the two of us at the heart of our relationship and household. We are knitting our own quilt of customs and practices. Hopefully the mosaic of old and new we're creating will be passed down for the next generation to add to and maybe do some of their own unraveling of the imperfections patching it in a new, more modern way. It's about creating a unique, colorful, meaningful patchwork of the traditional and the contemporary, and turning it into your own masterpiece, together, as a team.

Note: You might need to do some prior preparation for the small bonding challenge. Read the instructions and plan accordingly (try to keep your choices a secret from each other as you prepare).

Date Night Questions

Nostalgia and Upbringing

1. What is the first thing that comes to mind about your upbringing when you hear the following words:

    a. Smell

    _____

    b. Taste

    _____

    c. Touch

    _____

    d. Morning

    _____

    e. Sports

    _____

    f. Play

    _____

    g. Listen

    _____

h. Laughter

_____

i. Drama

_____

j. Learn

_____

k. Unlearn

_____

2. A tradition or practice that's important to you to keep going from your youth (can be something that you want to start again or something you already do). What about this tradition or practice is so important to you?

_____

_____

_____

_____

_____

3. Something unique about your upbringing that you don't think many other kids experienced in the same way you did:

_____

_____

_____

_____

_____

_____

4. A tradition or practice that we've started that's important to
   you that we keep doing. Why is it important to you?

_____

_____

_____

_____

_____

5. Answer the following from when you were younger. Favorite:

   a. Movie

_____

   b. TV Show

_____

c. Album

_____

d. Toy

_____

e. Character

_____

f. Teacher

_____

g. Neighbor

_____

h. Snack

_____

i. Family member

_____

j. Friend

_____

6. As we're constantly working to create the best "home," what elements would you love to emulate from those in which you grew up, or what elements would you like to avoid? Think about decor, mood, tone, rules, beliefs, etc.?

_____

_____

_____

_____

_____

_____

Nostalgia: Small Bonding Challenge

Each of you choose something from your youth that really holds a special place in your heart even if maybe it has been a long time since you practiced or experienced it. It might be a recipe, board game, art project, something you collected, and instrument, etc. Spend some time teaching one another or learning together about it. Cook it, play it, make it, etc.

OR

Think about an older member of your family who's still living. Come up with 10-20 questions together that you would like to ask this person about their life that you might not already know. Pick a time to interview this person with the questions you created, and record it. Ask them a tradition they would like you to keep going even after they are gone. You can even ask them some of the date night questions that you just asked one another!

You're Not Too Old, and It's Not Too Late

Everything about the night in February of 2018, when I went to Adam with the idea for the Marriage and Martinis podcast is a big blur. One thing I know for sure is that I expected him to tell me how crazy an idea it was. I expected to say I was joking (I actually was half joking). The whole conversation should have lasted less than a minute. Except that he said yes. In that moment, he chose hope over fear. He chose to believe in us even if it meant taking an absurd risk. It was definitely a "sliding doors" moment.

Our future depended on trusting that we needed to do something totally uncomfortable and new to change the course of our future. The odds were against us. We were 40-years-old. We had zero experience in podcasting. We were not in a great place financially or emotionally to take on such an endeavor. And yet, here we are, two- and-a-half years later, in the best place we've ever been in life.

There are all kinds of "crazy" things we have thought of doing or even done over the years. There are far-fetched dreams and goals that I still very much want to attempt. Now, I have the confidence to bring those ideas up in conversation and not worry that Adam is going to laugh.

Rather, he'll be my partner in trying to figure out how to make it all happen, and I'll do the same for him. That level of trust and communication has been a game-changer for our relationship: in our daily interactions, in parenting, and even in the bedroom. Reaction in the moment can have a true domino effect, so let's all pause and let questions and ideas soak in before responding. Sometimes, the best ideas at first don't present as such.

Some things I still want to put out into the world and hope to experience: run the Big Sur marathon, have an intimate experience with a woman, do a boudoir shoot, get a tattoo (maybe by the time you're reading this I'll have my first one), go to one of those amazing hut resorts in the middle of the ocean in Bali (if you're on instagram you know what I'm talking about), and do ayahuasca with a shaman in Peru.

Some things Adam would love to experience: spending some time in the East Asian countries, experiencing their culture and food sky-diving (which I'm too chicken sh*t to actually do), learn carpentry, cross-country train tour of the US, play drums for a live Guns N' Roses, Metallica, Motley Crue, and Rush tour.

Date Night Questions

You're Not Too Old, and It's Not Too Late

1. What is one dream or goal you've never really told anyone or talked about in detail? No matter how far-fetched it might seem, I want to hear about it.

_____

_____

_____

_____

_____

2. What's holding you back from attaining that dream or goal? Is it something that you really would love to pursue if you could?

_____

_____

_____

_____

_____

3. What is one experience you absolutely want us to have together in life that we haven't yet? What is it about this one experience that you think would be so amazing for both of us to do together?

_____

_____

_____

_____

_____

4. Do you know anyone personally who took a huge leap and pursued their dreams? What was it and how did they do it? How did it work out?

_____

_____

_____

_____

_____

5. If you could go back to school to an exceptional program to study one subject more in depth, just for the absolute joy and

passion of learning about it, what would it be? What fascinates you so much about that subject? Is there anything interesting that you know about it already that you would like to share with me?

_____

_____

_____

_____

_____

_____

6. Would you like to experience any of the following together (if you've done it, cross it off or say whether you would like to do it again; if you've never heard of some of the items, research them together and discuss). Then, each of you add your own two that are not included on this list.

   a. Drive across country

   b. Help build a house with Habitat for Humanity

   c. Host a fundraiser together for a charity close to your heart

   d. Live in another city/country for a year

   e. Take a class together such as

   f. Take part in an ayahuasca ceremony

   g. Visit Hedonism together

   h. Dinner In The Dark experience

   i. Swim with the Great White Sharks

j. Cage of death (Australia with saltwater crocodiles)

k. Bungee Jump/Skydive

l. Go to the airport and hop on whatever flight is available to anywhere in the world

m. _____

n. _____

You're Not Old And It's Not Too Late Small Challenge:

Download a bucket list app (Bucket List Maker is a good one), start a notebook or joint google doc, name it, and start by putting a dozen experiences you still want to have together (and apart). Even if something is a "maybe," add it to the list and revisit it down the line. Choose ONE of those that seems realistic, and set a target date. Do some research about it and come up with a possible plan, and maybe even a tentative date on the calendar.

TOPIC NUMBER EIGHT

Kinks and Fetishes
For Beginners

Five years ago I would probably have just skipped over this section. If you want to, I totally understand. You might be thinking that Adam and I are these really crazy sexual exploration type couples. The truth is, experimentation in the bedroom is very new to us. Let me clarify that statement: well-planned, open-communication experimentation is new to us. There have been times over the years we had spontaneously decided, mid-lovemaking, to "spice it up," but those situations never ended well (for more on that, check out episode #38). Adam has never been much for talking about sex in any way other than a joking manner. I think for a long time we didn't feel comfortable talking about it. Also, I don't think either of us even realized we wanted more in the bedroom. Once the podcast started, we had no choice but to talk openly, to experts and between the two of us. Before we knew it, we were giving disclaimers at the beginning of episodes telling our family members not to listen because there was so much explicit talk about our sex life. Sexual communication, like anything else, takes practice. Even after all of the communication and experimentation, the two of us are still trying to gain the confidence to try new things. I'm still struggling with body confidence in the bedroom, and Adam still struggles with intimate talk inside the bedroom, even though he has gotten more courageous outside of it. For some couples, being sexually confident and adventurous comes completely naturally, which is awesome. We are not that couple. However, we are determined to keep trying new things and listening to one another about our desires.

Just recently, there was one night when the kids were actually sleeping out, and Adam had planned a whole night of sexually-focused games to play together. When he first told me this was his plan for the evening, I was borderline angry. I had been so excited to relax on the couch in my cozy, ripped sweatpants and see how many Doritos I could fit into my mouth all night. But after telling me how much he had been looking forward to having some fun together and how much planning he had done (this was not exactly true....he bought a deck of cards), I finally agreed reluctantly.

After over twenty years together, we played strip poker for the first time, followed by naked Truth or Dare. At first, I was beyond uncomfortable. Getting naked and STAYING naked in front of Adam, let alone in a seated position (arguably the worst position for body folds and crevices we usually keep hidden), seemed far too daunting. But once I let go of all of that and got into the mindset that he wanted to do these things with me, what followed was one of the most fun, bonding, trusting nights we'd ever had.

And guess what? The folds, imperfections, and scars faded away in the beauty and excitement of the moment. Never did I think that would happen. Who knew that a night of games and nudity was exactly what I needed? I certainly did not. I am so glad I said yes.

Date Night Questions

Kinks and Fetishes For Beginners

1. Do you feel completely comfortable to share with me any-thing you've wanted to try in the bedroom that may not be part of our regular intimacy routine?

_____

_____

_____

_____

_____

2. What is one sexual experience in (or out of) the bedroom you would be interested in learning more about, together?

_____

_____

_____

_____

3. What's your biggest fear about trying something new in the bedroom and how could I make you feel more comfortable?

_____

_____

_____

_____

_____

4. What is something we've tried in the bedroom that took more courage than usual? How did it go? Would you want to try it again, and if so what can we do to make that interaction even better next time? If you don't want to try that again, why not, and what might you like to do instead?

_____

_____

_____

_____

_____

5. How can I make you feel more confident sexually?

_____

_____

_____

_____

_____

_____

_____

6. A common practice in the kink community is "aftercare" (taking care of one another in a sensitive and loving way). Some therapists argue that aftercare should be done more often in relationships between couples, not just after an intense sexual scene. What kind of aftercare do you wish we had more of in our relationship? What actions or words would you want to increase between us?

_____

_____

_____

_____

_____

The Kinks for beginners
Small Challenge

Each partner fills out this yes/no/maybe checklist and then you discuss your answers (if you've already experienced some of these then you can decide whether or not you would like to try it again). Take the time to research anything together about which you are uncertain or think might be interesting to try (actually, researching can be half the fun).

**Researching each act is highly recommended and encouraged before experimenting.

**Kinks and sexual experimentation is extremely subjective, and what may be considered, "vanilla" to one couple might be "risque" to another. The "yes, no, maybe checklists" are meant to figure out which acts you might want to research and look into in the future. Do whichever checklist feels more in your zone of comfort, or of course do both if that appeals to you. Note: just because you put a yes does not mean you have to try it. It's a starting point for discussion and research.

	YES	NO	MAYBE
Play strip poker	☐	☐	☐
Play truth or dare	☐	☐	☐
Create a "sex song playlist" together	☐	☐	☐
Try CBD-infused sexual products (check out Folia) Sext each other one time each week	☐	☐	☐
Schedule to meet in the middle of the day for a quickie	☐	☐	☐
Exchange massages	☐	☐	☐
Take a bubble bath together	☐	☐	☐
Go to a strip club or burlesque show (research your local city)	☐	☐	☐
Listen to audio erotica (check out an app such as Dipsea)	☐	☐	☐
Get tied up	☐	☐	☐
Try a new lube Keep the lights on	☐	☐	☐
Dirty talk (discuss what might turn you on)	☐	☐	☐
Tie up your partner	☐	☐	☐
Sensory play with food	☐	☐	☐

	YES	NO	MAYBE
Sensory play with texture	☐	☐	☐
Hot candle wax (find a candle made specifically for sensory play)	☐	☐	☐
Blindfold Wartenberg Wheel	☐	☐	☐
Fin (finger) vibrator	☐	☐	☐
Spanking	☐	☐	☐
Sex in a public place (if so, where?)	☐	☐	☐
Enact a dom/sub roleplay	☐	☐	☐
Costume roleplay	☐	☐	☐
"Pick one another up" in a bar	☐	☐	☐
Read a book/take a workshop together on tantric sex.	☐	☐	☐
Spicier Spice (feel free to skip this one or wait to revisit it in the future)	☐	☐	☐
Mutual masturbation	☐	☐	☐
Watch porn (try female-centered, female-directed porn like Erika Lust)	☐	☐	☐
Explore having a threesome	☐	☐	☐
Purchase handcuffs	☐	☐	☐

	YES	NO	MAYBE
Purchase a vibrator together	☐	☐	☐
Purchase a cock ring (try the JE JOUE)	☐	☐	☐
Door Jam Cuffs	☐	☐	☐
Sex Swing	☐	☐	☐

	YES	NO	MAYBE
Play strip poker	☐	☐	☐
Play truth or dare	☐	☐	☐
Create a "sex song playlist" together	☐	☐	☐
Try CBD-infused sexual products (check out Folia) Sext each other one time each week	☐	☐	☐
Schedule to meet in the middle of the day for a quickie	☐	☐	☐
Exchange massages	☐	☐	☐
Take a bubble bath together	☐	☐	☐
Go to a strip club or burlesque show (research your local city)	☐	☐	☐
Listen to audio erotica (check out an app such as Dipsea)	☐	☐	☐
Get tied up	☐	☐	☐
Try a new lube Keep the lights on	☐	☐	☐
Dirty talk (discuss what might turn you on)	☐	☐	☐
Tie up your partner	☐	☐	☐
Sensory play with food	☐	☐	☐

	YES	NO	MAYBE
Sensory play with texture	☐	☐	☐
Hot candle wax (find a candle made specifically for sensory play)	☐	☐	☐
Blindfold Wartenberg Wheel	☐	☐	☐
Fin (finger) vibrator	☐	☐	☐
Spanking	☐	☐	☐
Sex in a public place (if so, where?)	☐	☐	☐
Enact a dom/sub roleplay	☐	☐	☐
Costume roleplay	☐	☐	☐
"Pick one another up" in a bar	☐	☐	☐
Read a book/take a workshop together on tantric sex.	☐	☐	☐
Spicier Spice (feel free to skip this one or wait to revisit it in the future)	☐	☐	☐
Mutual masturbation	☐	☐	☐
Watch porn (try female-centered, female-directed porn like Erika Lust)	☐	☐	☐
Explore having a threesome	☐	☐	☐
Purchase handcuffs	☐	☐	☐

	YES	NO	MAYBE
Purchase a vibrator together	☐	☐	☐
Purchase a cock ring (try the JE JOUE)	☐	☐	☐
Door Jam Cuffs	☐	☐	☐
Sex Swing	☐	☐	☐

Keeping Up With The Joneses

Adam's and my relationship with finances and spending was dysfunctional for a long time. I like to say "was," because the first step is admitting it. We have done that part. Without taking everyone down a rabbit hole of all our poor choices (there are plenty of podcast episodes you can listen to about that), I'll give you a little of the "Adam and Danielle Greatest Hits" (spoiler alert: none of these choices were great).

When Adam and I first started dating (the second time), I was in college in New York City. I was living on Ramen Noodles and cigarettes, but Adam was already working in his family business making an income. I was in awe of the way he would overtip waiters, take cabs instead of subways, and shopped in stores from which I only dreamt of buying. I was enamored by the way he spent money with such ease. It was different than anything I had ever experienced. It felt liberating. I got used to this style of living very quickly.

Indulgence (and overindulgence) had once played a big role in our life together. Throwing lavish parties, over-the-top shopping excursions, and weekly dinners at nice restaurants kept life exciting and fun. If we were struggling in our marriage or stressed out by anything life threw our way, debauchery was a great distraction. No matter what was happening in the realistic realm, we could evade it by escaping to a dreamier version of life.

Once our kids were born, we should have realized that it was time to start conserving. But since spending had become our form of "therapy," and parenting only adds stress to the equation, our spending only got worse. We didn't know how to exist together on a budget. Five years into our marriage, a new neighborhood was being built in our town. The houses were overwhelmingly enormous and beautiful. Adam became obsessed with moving us there. He crunched numbers into spreadsheets and constantly justified why we should move. For over a year we fought about that house. Ultimately, I didn't want to be resented by Adam, and I agreed to move there. It didn't take six months before Adam realized what a mistake we had made. Not only could we not afford this home, but the appeal of "the chase" wore off quickly.

I held my own portion of responsibility as we headed down our financial spiral. After being married for around ten years, I noticed that so many women my age were getting engagement ring upgrades. I wanted one, too. I dropped not-so-subtle hints for around a year. Adam eventually bought me a much bigger, shinier diamond. Similar to the way the house quickly lost its sexiness for Adam once we moved in, I quickly realized that the reasons I had coveted this ring were absurd. We couldn't afford it, and while it was gorgeous, it only added to my feelings of guilt and unhappiness. I sold the ring six months later.

Discovering what truly fulfills Adam and me has been an ongoing journey. Starting the podcast led us on a different type of adventure, redirecting our energy in a way that was more constructive. We both definitely possess a more wild side to us, but the key has been to find forms of excitement that are void of the danger and chaos attached to a more debaucherous lifestyle. Fun takes on a different meaning in our lives now. We still indulge, but we're able to do it within the confines of our financial limitations. I'm proud of how far we've come in terms of forming alternate paths to gratification, and how we've worked together to get here. We're no longer trying to prove our success with overwhelming houses or expensive jewelry (not that there's anything wrong with those types of purchases, at all, as long as someone can afford them). We're figuring out what fills us up and makes us feel alive and invigorated. It's been such a wild ride, and I can't wait to see where it takes us next.

Date Night Questions

Keeping Up With The Joneses

1. How were money and finances discussed and treated in your household growing up?

_____

_____

_____

_____

_____

_____

2. Were you taught anything about saving, budgeting, stocks, etc. growing up? If so, by whom and what did they teach you?

_____

_____

_____

_____

3. The first purchase you remember making with your own money that really meant something to you?

_____

_____

_____

_____

4. A large purchase you've made that wound up being disappointing?

_____

_____

_____

5. Something you've always wanted to buy but is completely impractical?

_____

_____

_____

_____

6. Has your view of money and finances changed over the years? If so, how?

_____

_____

_____

_____

_____

_____

7. Do you feel like we're a team when it comes to figuring out our finances, budgeting, and decision making on how we save and spend our money? What's one way we are succeeding/ something we are doing well in terms of finances?

_____

_____

_____

_____

_____

_____

_____

8. How could we be more of a team? What would you like us to start doing concerning our money and finances that we're not currently doing?

_____

_____

_____

_____

_____

_____

9. What's one way we've followed our own path in life and our marriage rather than being influenced by others, simply because it works for us?

_____

_____

_____

_____

_____

_____

_____

10. What's one way you think we've been influenced by our peers and got sucked in to "keeping up with the joneses?"

_____

_____

_____

_____

11. A way we're finding fulfillment as a couple that doesn't involve a lot of spending:

_____

_____

_____

_____

12. Something specific you would love for us to save for in our future for which we are not currently?

_____

_____

_____

_____

13. Who do you admire in terms of how they manage their money and spending (family members, friends, neighbors)?

_____

_____

_____

_____

_____

_____

14. Would it make sense to do any of the following together:

    a. Read a book about finance and discuss (Check out "Nudge." "Worth It," or "Get Good With Money").

    b. Download a couples' finance app such as Zeta.

    c. Hire a financial planner.

_____

_____

_____

_____

_____

Small Challenge:

First, put this list in order (each of you, separately) from least important to most important in terms of finances. Feel free to add specific information to each category and personalize each item more, making it more applicable to your situation and lifestyle. Also, two have been left blank for each of you to fill in. After you've compared lists and discussed them, create a mission statement together about how you're going to work as a team in terms of finances.

Bonus: Laminate two copies of that mission statement, and each of you keep it in your wallet, phone card holder, or somewhere you can be reminded of your shared goals and values.

1. Travel

2. Entertainment/recreation

3. Education/continuing education

4. Physical and mental health

5. Philanthropy/charity

6. Cars

7. Home projects/renovation/decorating

8. Luxury goods (jewelry, accessories, non-necessity technology, wine, jewelry etc.)

9. _____

10. _____

Stuff I Want You To Know

Recently, I asked Adam a question that had been on my mind: "Can you name a podcast, TV show, movie, or album that you love that is created by or features strong females as the main focus?" The answer was exactly as I expected. "No." A lot of partners probably wouldn't mind this answer. After all, why should I really care if the shows he watches or music he plays contain a focus on strong women? However, it did bother me. How could he truly appreciate the female experience and be empathetic and compassionate towards the needs of me and our daughter if he's only surrounding himself with the masculine perspective and experience? I knew that this was something I really wanted him to start focusing on even a little more. Studying the history of and fighting for women's rights has always been a huge passion of mine. It was even my major in college! It's not that Adam doesn't believe this is important. But I had come to the realization of how beneficial it would be if he had a firsthand understanding of why it's so important to help empower women, and teach our sons to do the same. He's appreciative of the subject on a passive level, when it would mean so much to me that he takes a more active stance.

On the other hand, Adam has long been frustrated that I don't understand anything about savings, the mortgage, or other aspects of finance that affect our life. I spent a long time making little to no effort to learn about this, both because it scared me and because I really just have zero interest. Looking back, I realize how selfish I was. He had hinted so many times that he would love my input into our finances and how we chose to spend our money. But I ignored those hints, causing a lot of built-up resentment and disconnect between us. Taking a more active role in this aspect of our life together has cultivated a closeness between us that's gratifying in a way that did not exist before in our relationship.

Having a partner who shows concern about aspects of life that are important to us, stressful to us, or in which we take pride, is meaningful and sparks a different understanding of and appreciation for one another. If Adam takes even half an hour a week to invest his time and attention into a show that portrays strong female characters, or listens to an album on his way to work by a powerful female vocal artist with empowering lyrics, he may become more sensitive and empathetic to different
versions of the human experience. Likewise, if I take more time to understand the intricacies of our finances, I'll have more concern and mindfulness about a big source of his stress, therefore being better equipped to help ease his worries. Plus, how awesome would it be for the kids to see their dad belting out Beyonce at the top of his lungs during a car ride, and to see their mom working hard to overcome her overwhelming fear of math as a means to help their dad? It's never too late to take a more active role in significant aspects of each other's lives. It can absolutely strengthen your bond as an ever-changing, ever-evolving couple.

Date Night Questions

Stuff I Want You To Know

1. What are three aspects of life right now that you truly enjoy?

_____

_____

_____

2. Is there an area of our life together about which you wish I would become more knowledgeable so we could work together more in the decision-making process and share responsibility?

_____

_____

_____

_____

3. Is there a social issue about which you feel passionate that you wish our family would be more charitable and show more concern? What about this issue is so important to you?

_____

_____

_____

_____

_____

4. If I could learn more about one topic, or understand and appreciate on a deeper level, what would it be? How do you think I would benefit from learning more about this? How do you think our relationship would benefit?

_____

_____

_____

_____

_____

5. Something about your past: a person, experience, achievement, etc. that meant a lot to you but maybe I don't know as much about as you wish? Tell me more about it.

_____

_____

_____

_____

_____

6. Name one of each of the following that you would love me to experience so I could have a better understanding and appreciation for it:

   a. Book/Podcast

   _____

   b. TV Show

   _____

   c. Movie

   _____

   d. Album

   _____

7. On the other hand, is there anything in life that you absolutely love indulging in without any interference? Something that is just "yours?" A hobby, aspect of work, activity?

   _____

   _____

   _____

   _____

   _____

   _____

Small Challenge: Stuff I Want You To Know

Each of you pick a topic about which you're knowledgeable and/or passionate, which your partner is not quite as much. On a piece of paper, google docs, or notes, etc., create a ten question quiz for the other person about this subject. Feel free to use google docs for help (but they must be questions to which you already know the answers). Exchange quizzes and fill them out, then give them back to be graded. See who gets a higher score.

Bonus: Come up with a prize for the winner, whoever gets a higher score on their quiz.

Fun and Games

During Quarantine, my family started having what our kids call, "fun nights." Honestly, these are really just unstructured nights when we all hang out together. Some nights wind up with a movie, some with Adam teaching the kids how to play poker or blackjack, and others are just with us putting on music and acting silly and crazy.

Especially in the midst of a pandemic, we all need a break from the stress and rigidity. Sometimes we need to purely unwind, with no pressure, no responsibilities, and no end goal other than to laugh, and be in the moment. These nights are equally as important for us as for the kids. Sometimes, the most productive thing we can do for our relationships, whether it be with our spouse, friends, or kids, is to be completely unproductive; to just be in the moment with zero expectations except enjoyment. It's so much harder to do than it seems. We can all think back to a time when we felt pure joy. Sometimes it means channeling our inner teenager who was selfish and self- indulgent enough to forget the world around us and our responsibilities, and just immerse ourselves in the moment.

Date Night Questions

Fun and Games

1. Most fun night we have ever had together?

_____

_____

_____

_____

_____

_____

2. Most fun you ever had without me?

_____

_____

_____

_____

_____

_____

3. Most fun memory from your youth?

_____

_____

_____

_____

_____

4. When was the last time you felt pure joy without any under-
   lying stress?

_____

_____

_____

_____

_____

5. Something other people find fun that you find to be
   overrated?

_____

_____

_____

_____

6. Something that looks fun that you still want to experience?

_____

_____

_____

_____

_____

7. Who is your go-to person for complete and utter fun (besides me)?

_____

_____

_____

_____

_____

Just For Fun

(Turn this into a drinking game, or just play for fun).

Never Have I ever Couples' edition:

1. Pretended to be asleep so that we didn't have to have sex

   _____

2. Hid a purchase/packages from you because I didn't want you to know about them.

   _____

3. Faked an orgasm

   _____

4. Waited for the last second before you got home to do the housework

   _____

5. Spent longer in the bathroom just to have more alone time

   _____

6. Sat in the driveway or a parking lot scrolling social media just so I didn't have to go home yet

   _____

7. Gone ahead and watched a show even though I said I would wait for you

_____

8. Argued with you even though I knew you were right just so I didn't have to admit it

_____

9. Waited til we were done having sex to go masterbate and finish

_____

10. Pretended I couldn't do something so I wouldn't have to

_____

Would You Rather:

1. Swim naked in a pool or the ocean?

_____

2. Have a romantic weekend in a house on a lake or a resort on the beach?

_____

3. Top or Bottom?

4. Scalp massage or foot massage?

5. Read the book or watch the movie?

6. Go out dancing or sing karaoke?

7. Superpower: read minds or fly?

8. All you can eat sushi or greasy appetizers?

9. Be on the cover of Time Magazine or Rolling Stone Magazine?

10. Nobel Peace Prize or Academy Award?

11. Walk a mile or run a mile?

12. Give your dog a human name or a "pet" name?

_____

13. Vodka or tequila?

_____

14. Sleep in late or nap?

_____

15. Give up coffee or wine?

_____

Small Bonding Challenge

What's something you used to do for fun in the beginning of your relationship that you haven't done in a long time? (For Adam and me, it was going out and playing pool in a pub). Figure out how to participate in that activity again, whether it be a game you played, a place you frequented, or another activity. If you are able, find a way to do that thing tonight. If not, plan the steps and schedule the activity for sometime ASAP.

The Future's So Bright

There have been a few times in my life when I lost all hope. The first was at 27-years- old, when I was suffering from a debilitating bout of obsessive-compulsive disorder. I was married, pregnant and moved back into my childhood bedroom at my parents' house while they nursed me back to health. I was an empty, lifeless vessel in full survival mode. The sights, sounds, and tastes that had once brought me so much joy suddenly felt like nothing more than annoying distractions. Thankfully, as many terrible times do, this crisis did pass. With so much support, therapy, and the right dose of medication, I was able to once again enjoy life. In fact, my gratitude since that time has increased daily in many ways. Every time I can leave the house and not partake in "right-amount actions," eat food without worrying that it's contaminated, or get a full night of sleep without waking up in a panic, I take a moment and really appreciate how far I've come.

The second bout with hopelessness was around the time we started the podcast. Adam was indulging in what he refers to as, "escapism." He would leave for extended periods of time, drinking heavily, gambling with money we didn't have, all while refusing to communicate about why this was happening. I was married to a man I didn't recognize, and I had a marriage in which I wasn't sure I could stay. People refer to "rock bottom" as if it's this sharp, defined bottom that can be remembered as a solitary moment in time. Our rock bottom lasted a few years, and at first, we crawled out of it, slowly, testing the waters to see if progressing side by side was even an option for us anymore. Had we separated, maybe we would both be content living our separate lives. I do believe in separation. I believe in making hard choices required to close the door to toxicity and open another to happiness. We somehow found a way to make the most of life again, together. We did not bounce back. It has been an ongoing process involving so much hard work, gratitude, communication and commitment: coffee dates on the weekend to discuss life, therapy, both apart and together, and listening to one another through raw, real conversations on almost 200 podcast episodes over the course of two and a half years.

It has not been easy. But "hard" does not necessarily mean "bad." We've done the tough, messy, tedious work. I'm so damn proud of us. I can now say with certainty that if I had another bout with OCD, Adam would be the one nursing me back to health this time. Adam no longer needs to practice "escapism," because I'm here, finally sharing the financial burdens, and being his partner completely, rather than just choosing areas in which I feel comfortable being involved.

The goal is to be ever-evolving, learning, thriving human beings, both individually and as a team. That means that we can never settle, thinking we somehow know everything about one another. Complacency is not the objective. Passion, adventure, fun, laughter, support, emotion, and fulfillment are the intentions. Esther Perel says that it is possible to have several marriages or relationships with the same person, constantly recreating your bond. I find so much excitement in that thought. So here's to the next conversation, the next intimate encounter, the next constructive disagreement, the next fit of joint laughter, the next passionate apology, and the mysterious limitless future right in front of us. Cheers to discovering one another all over again, a million times more.

Date Night Questions

The Future's So Bright

1. Five years from this point right now, I hope I can look back and have accomplished these three things:

_____

_____

_____

_____

_____

2. One way I would love to grow emotionally over the next five years is:

_____

_____

_____

_____

_____

3. One way I would love to grow intellectually and/or spiritually over the next five years is:

_____

_____

_____

_____

_____

4. Two ways I hope our relationship continues to grow and thrive are:

_____

_____

_____

_____

_____

5. Something I can do more consistently to help nurture our relationship and connection is:

_____

_____

_____

_____

6. Something I hope we can work on and argue/disagree about less in the near future is:

_____

_____

_____

_____

_____

7. One way I am going to contribute to arguing and disagreeing less about this issue is to:

_____

_____

_____

_____

8. Besides our relationship, a relationship I would love to nurture and invest more time and energy into is:

_____

_____

_____

_____

9. Trip and or experience I hope we can start saving and planning for soon is:

_____

_____

_____

_____

_____

10. Habit and/or tradition I would like us to practice more consistently in our household is:

_____

_____

_____

_____

11. Something charitable and/or a social issue I would love to get more involved in in the near future:

_____

_____

_____

_____

Small Bonding Challenge

This is the final challenge of the book. That means all of your creativity, thoughtfulness, vulnerability, and open-mindedness has led to this endeavor. We hope you'll take some time to savor this activity and use it as a catalyst to inspire the actions, commitment, and mind-set from this point forward.

Find a large container that can be sealed tightly. This will be your time capsule which you'll bury together or hide somewhere safe to be dug up or retrieved on the date of your choice sometime in the future (a year from now, five years from now, etc.) Make sure you mark a calendar or somehow solidify an official opening date. Each of you can write your own letter to put inside to one another (you can read it to each other now or keep it a secret to read only when you open the capsule), or you can write a letter together. You can also print out this topic's date night questions (or any topic that feels relevant to your goals and dreams right now), answer those questions on paper, and put them inside the capsule. Basically, what you include in there is something for you to decide together, and there are no rules or limitations.

Conclusion

One thing that's on my bucket list in the near future is to get my first tattoo. It sounds so cliche, but I've thought about it for a long time, The fear of doing something so permanent has kept me from going through with it. I am a constantly changing work-in- progress, and making a statement that will stay with me forever regardless of how I'll transform and develop seems impetuous. But isn't there also something significant about looking at that tattoo for the rest of my life and, regardless of whether the design continues to accurately match my persona ten or twenty years down the road, remembering that at one point, it was meaningful to me? It signifies a moment in time when those words or symbols were so important to me that I had it indelibly marked upon my body. We have a tendency to want to filter precisely which decisions, moments, failures, successes and relationships to recollect in our lives. It's like reconstructing a story without the embarrassing or hurtful chapters, because that version is easier and less humiliating to share. People have asked Adam and me, "how are you going to feel if your children one day listen to your podcast and hear all the horrible choices you made?" Like a tattoo, all of our decisions, actions and struggles have become a permanent mark on our lives, and we have decided to look back and move forward while embracing all aspects of our story.

I want all those conversations Adam and I have had out there forever. Because they are ours. And no matter how far we've come and the lessons we've learned, those messy, chaotic discussions still mark a point in time when we embraced ourselves and all of our flaws, rather than picking and choosing which aspects of our relationship we deemed "worthy" enough to reveal. There is no doubt that we are very imperfect people. We have almost two hundred episodes of evidence to prove it. But, do you know how liberating that has been, documenting our own true story through honest conversations? I say, keep the dialogue going. Be raw. Be honest. Be flawed. Be your perfectly imperfect selves. Write down your answers in a journal. Keep the evidence. Share it, don't share it, whatever you decide. Just don't be afraid of it. This is your story. Every masterpiece has several drafts. So, this was your first draft, or maybe it was your fifth draft. From here, go forward and start making the necessary edits. Write new chapters. Get support from people you trust. Lean in to the messiness. In the end, you can't have a bestseller without going through all steps of the process, first.

Notes

CPSIA information can be obtained
at www.ICGtesting.com
Printed in the USA
LVHW051214100223
738841LV00005B/9